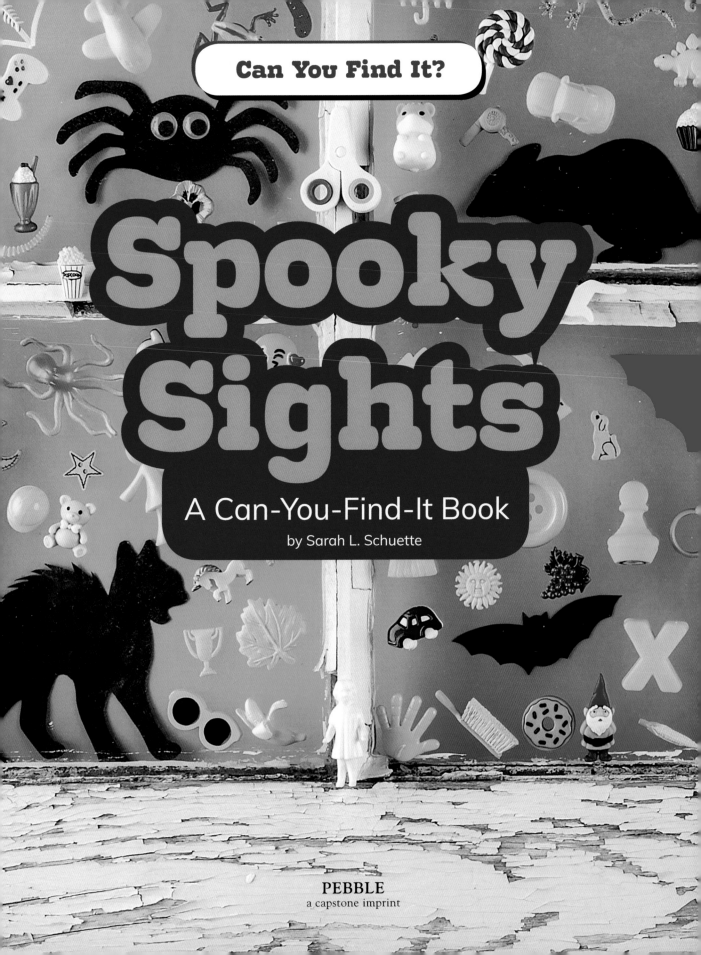

Can You Find It?

Spooky Sights

A Can-You-Find-It Book

by Sarah L. Schuette

PEBBLE

a capstone imprint

Eye See You!

Can you find
these things?

 candy

 fish bones

 red pepper

 star

ONE WAY →

 wand   pig   dragonfly   tongs   pineapple   cupcake

Full Moon

Can you find
these things?

witch
hat

tire

horseshoe

sword

watermelon

oar

airplane

dragon

alligator

grill

Zombie Lunch

Can you find
these things?

 book

 flamingo

 eggplant

 butterfly

snake

toaster

blender

light bulb

rainbow

pickle

Boo!

Can you find these things?

 hand

 corn cob

 wizard hat

 grapes

mushroom

palm
tree

race
car

snowflake

tractor

cactus

Haunted House

Can you find these things?

 balloon

 pencil

 chicken

 snowman

 penguin

 trophy

 comb

 hair dryer

 bone

 arrow

Skeleton Dance

Can you find these things?

 umbrella   strawberry   hanger   cow

 skunk   hot dog   sunglasses   basketball   snake   seahorse

Monster Mouths

Can you find these things?

drill

koala

stapler

globe

paintbrush

shell

rabbit

knife

mitten

scooter

Mummy Madness

Can you find these things?

 lion

 swan

 football

 donut

ladder

chef's
hat

french
fries

rooster

clothespin

dog

Jack-o-Lanterns

Can you find these things?

teddy bear

starfish

bananas

gnome

 taco

 candy corn

 rubber duck

 soda

 ninja

 tiger

Spells and Potions

Can you find
these things?

 pretzel

 turtle

 bat

 taxi

bowling
pin

bobber

bucket

calculator

peanut

skull

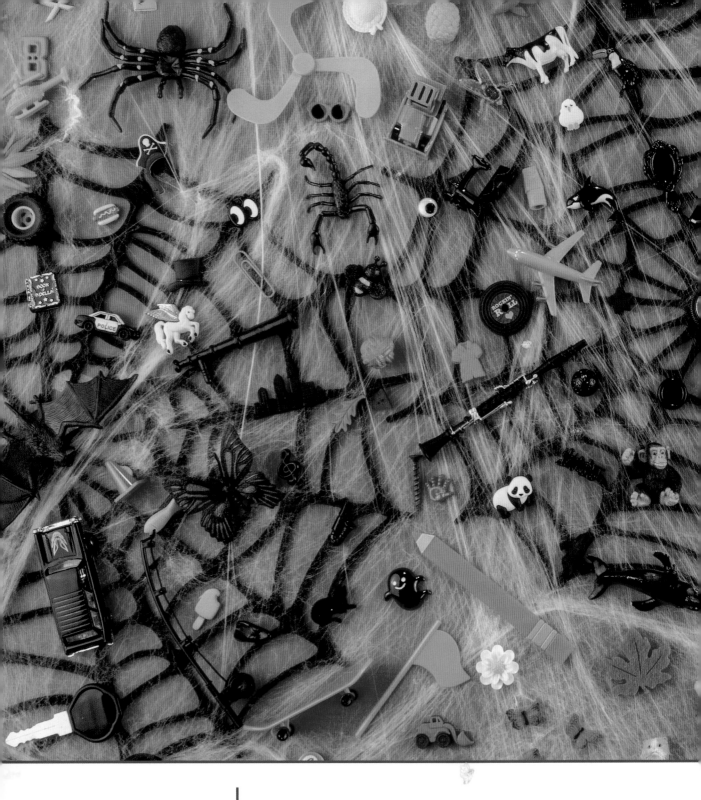

Webs

Can you find
these things?

octopus

pizza

fly

ice pop

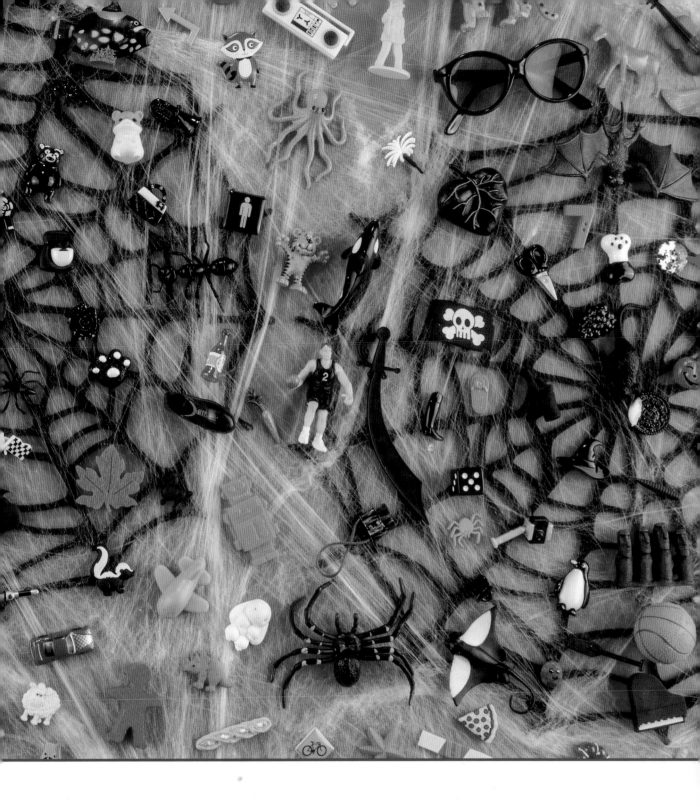

 helicopter

 shirt

 scissors

 panda

 traffic cone

 carrot

Wolves in the Woods

Can you find these things?

 hamburger

ax

 spoon

 shark

 camel

 pants

 rolling pin

 wrench

 zipper

 tent

Wicked Witch

Can you find these things?

ant

clarinet

compass

harp

 gorilla

 lobster

 mouse

 crown

 robot

 trash can

Infested!

Can you find
these things?

key

donkey

leaf

moon

PETTING ZOO

Turn the page for the answer key!

pumpkin

baseball bat

shoe

cat

crutch

snail

Psst! Did you know that Pebs the Pebble was hiding
in EVERY PUZZLE in this book?

It's true! Go back and look!

Look for other books in this series:

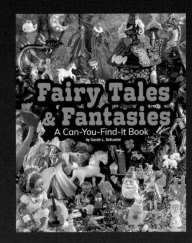

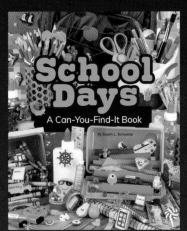

The author dedicates this book to the Harper Family.

Pebble Sprout is published by Pebble, an imprint of Capstone.
1710 Roe Crest Drive, North Mankato, Minnesota 56003
www.capstonepub.com

Library of Congress Cataloging-in-Publication Data is available on the Library of Congress website.
ISBN 978-1-9771-2256-8 (library binding)
ISBN 978-1-9771-2622-1 (paperback)
ISBN 978-1-9771-2308-4 (eBook PDF)

Summary: Lead kids on a tour of spooky sights! Zombies, witches, monsters, and other spine-chilling creatures make finding the hidden objects in the full-color photo puzzles a BOO-tastic challenge. Pictographs and word labels are included in each to-find list.

Image Credits
All photos by Capstone Studio: Karon Dubke

Editorial Credits
Shelly Lyons, editor; Heidi Thompson, designer; Marcy Morin, set stylist;
Morgan Walters, media researcher; Kathy McColley, production specialist

Printed and bound in China.
3322